Better Physical Fitness

Better Physical Fitness

David C. Cooke

With a foreword by D. Cyril Joynson, Principal Lecturer
Health Education, Monmouthshire Training College.

KAYE & WARD · LONDON
in association with
Hicks, Smith and Sons
Australia and New Zealand

First published in Great Britain
and the British Commonwealth by
NICHOLAS KAYE LIMITED
194-200 Bishopsgate, London EC2
1962

Second edition published by
Kaye & Ward Limited
194-200 Bishopsgate, London EC2
1971

ISBN 0 7182 0480 8

Printed offset in Great Britain by
STRAKER BROTHERS LTD
Bishopsgate, London, EC2

Contents

Acknowledgements

The author would like to extend his appreciation to Larry Abruzzesa, Michael Heron, and Jim Cooke, who spent many patient hours posing for the photographs on the following pages; Joe Weider, who has been called 'The Builder of Champions', for supplying sets of barbells and dumbbells; Raymond Heron, who offered valuable suggestions and knowledge gained from years of experience as a physical culturist; and Denny McMains, who not only designed the jacket but also supplied two fine anatomical drawings for reproduction. Without the co-operation of these people, this book would not have been possible in its present form.

To Ray Heron,
with thanks for many years of friendship

Foreword

The fact that young people of today are maturing physically much earlier than their predecessors adds emphasis to the need for a programme of functional and developmental exercise to encourage maximum and correct development during the final years of adolescence.

So often, after leaving school, one is not fortunate enough to have the opportunity of being a member of some organization where it is possible to take part in some form of physical activity. Such unlucky boys need another source. Again, keeping fit by playing games is enjoyable but this is only one aspect of physical development. Skill is enhanced by strength and mobility. It is now well established that muscular strength can be increased by progressive resistance exercise, so that training of this nature will benefit not only the games player but also those who, because they are employed in some sedentary occupation, are not developing their muscles by manual work. Similarly, exercises which stimulate circulation and respiration will help to revitalise the body. At the same time it should be noted that, as well as building up muscles, exercise can also reduce fat from those places where it is doing no good at all. By being really fit you will do justice to yourself in both work and play and will enjoy and perform them better accordingly.

The author of this book has made a valid point that suitable physical conditioning exercises can be practised in the privacy of the home, using equipment which is to hand, and using the bedroom and garden as the gymnasium. It is a helpful and skilful contribution.

In these circumstances the performer can exercise at his own rate and within his own limitations. It is unwise to attempt too much in one session and it is equally unwise to take part in vigorous physical activity at infrequent intervals. Bearing this in mind, and following the maxim of a little and often, you will find that short but regular sessions are invaluable.

The subject matter in the classified chapters is well illustrated and easy to follow. It has been limited to avoid the temptation to select too many activities in any one session and the performer must prepare his routine with this in mind. The exercises, however, can be made as strenuous as the performer wishes them to be and they are sufficiently interesting and challenging to stand repetition. These exercises which give all-round development are effective, and interest can be maintained by setting a target and increasing the load or the challenge.

This book may also appeal to those of us who are not so young but who would like to regain our boyish figures and vigour.

by D. Cyril Joynson,
Principal Lecturer Health Education,
Monmouthshire Training College.

Introduction

Physical fitness is something with which every person in the civilized world should be concerned – for his own good. No matter how much money a person may have or how many things he may possess during his lifetime, the only truly irreplaceable object he ever owns is his body. This should be reason enough for every boy to want to improve his physical fitness.

Years ago people thought of physical-fitness programmes solely as methods to develop bulging muscles and great power. Now, however, we know that a person can be physically fit without having bulging muscles, and we know that many other benefits come from regular participation in planned physical-education activities. We know that about 90 per cent of the backaches which plague people can be eliminated by proper exercise. We know that a physically fit person uses 40 per cent *less* energy to do the same work as one who is not fit, that a fit person is less susceptible to common injuries, that many heart diseases are the result of poor physical fitness, and that both nervous and emotional tensions can be reduced through regular physical activities.

Physical fitness is a problem which every person should want to solve by himself, for his own personal well-being. Then why don't more people exercise? Simply because they think it is hard work. Rather than being hard work, exercise is more fun, and more relaxing, than many of the things we do in daily life and call fun!

The exercises described and illustrated on the following pages were planned expressly for boys. Yet the same exercises can be done by adults, and with the same beneficial results. So why not get your father or elder brother to work them out *with* you? No one is ever too old to begin and follow a regular exercise programme.

DAVID C. COOKE

How Fit Should You Be?

You have probably noticed that once or twice a year your father has a service station mechanic put new spark plugs and distributor points in the family automobile, and that he watches the mileage carefully to see when the next oil change is due. You also know why he does these things. An automobile is a machine, and it will not operate to its full level of efficiency unless it is given care.

But did you ever stop to think that your body is also a machine, and that it, too, requires a certain amount of care if it is expected to operate as well as possible? Unfortunately, many people actually abuse their bodies through neglect far more than they would ever abuse an automobile or a vacuum cleaner or a washing machine. And while any other machine used in daily life can be replaced when it wears out, the body can never be replaced.

Before you try to set up an exercise programme for yourself, bear in mind that heredity and health determine the top limit to which your physical capacity can be developed. This limit is generally referred to as your 'potential physical capacity', and it varies from person to person. Most of us, for example, could train for a lifetime and never come close to running a four-minute mile, simply because our bodies are not built for it.

The top limit at which you can perform physically right now is called your 'acquired capacity', because it is strength and stamina which have been acquired or developed through physical activity in your daily routines. There is a world of difference between acquired capacity and

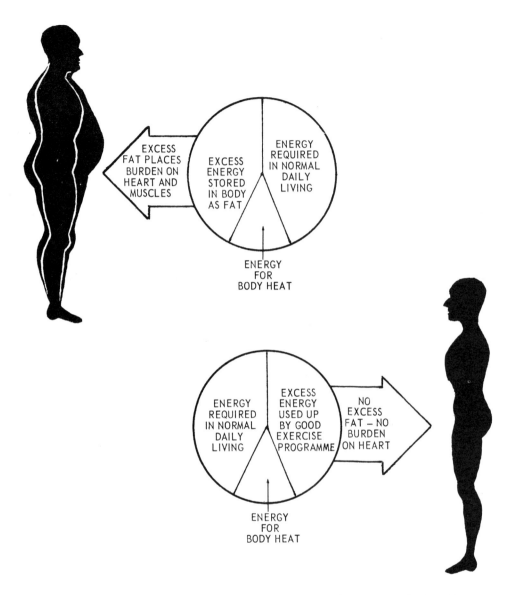

EXCESS FAT PLACES BURDEN ON HEART AND MUSCLES

EXCESS ENERGY STORED IN BODY AS FAT

ENERGY REQUIRED IN NORMAL DAILY LIVING

ENERGY FOR BODY HEAT

ENERGY REQUIRED IN NORMAL DAILY LIVING

EXCESS ENERGY USED UP BY GOOD EXERCISE PROGRAMME

NO EXCESS FAT – NO BURDEN ON HEART

ENERGY FOR BODY HEAT

When a person is overweight, he has more fat in his body than is good for him. Fat makes the heart work harder, since each extra pound of body fat requires approximately a quarter of a mile of blood vessels.

potential capacity. The physical capacity of the average person who does not follow a regular exercise programme is between 16 and 27 per cent of his potential; these figures can be *doubled* through proper exercise.

According to studies made by the United States Air Force School of Aviation Medicine, men who have put their bodies into proper physical condition through a planned exercise programme are able to think faster and more clearly, do not tire as easily, and even have more ambition to study longer hours than those who are not in good condition. Harvard and other universities have also discovered that the best athletes are often the best students as well.

These studies prove beyond question that physical conditioning does more for the body than merely harden the muscles and that a boy or a man whose muscles are in good shape is generally in a far better position to face the problems of daily life.

Physical conditioning, then, is something for which everyone should strive. But, as with all things that are worth having, it does not come easily. A certain amount of work is necessary, just as a certain amount of work is necessary to keep an automobile in good condition.

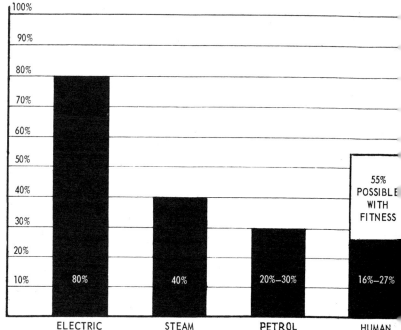

Efficiency of the human body compares poorly with a modern machine, but it can be improved by exercise.

How Your Muscles Work

The human body is made up mainly of bone, muscle, and fat, with 639 different muscles accounting for about 45 per cent of the body weight. Some of these are called *voluntary muscles*, and others are referred to as *involuntary muscles*. Voluntary muscles are the ones we control consciously – like those in our arms and legs and neck. Involuntary muscles are the ones we do not control consciously – like those in the heart, intestines, stomach, and blood vessels.

All of these various muscles are composed of thread-like fibres, many of which are so small and thin that they can be seen only with a microscope. Some small muscles, such as those in the eyes, are made up of as few as eight of these tiny fibres, while large muscles are composed of tens of thousands of muscle fibres. Doctors have estimated that there are about two hundred and fifty million muscle fibres in the body.

Each fibre in a muscle is surrounded by tiny blood vessels called *capillaries*. With a microscope you can see that a piece of muscle tissue as thin as the lead in a pencil may contain as many as four hundred capillaries. These tiny blood vessels supply the muscles with a constant supply of oxygen and food and also remove waste products.

Most of the voluntary muscles are connected to bones by cords of white tissue called *tendons*. The attachment of a muscle to the bone which it moves is called the *insertion*; the attachment to the bone which it does not move is called the *origin*.

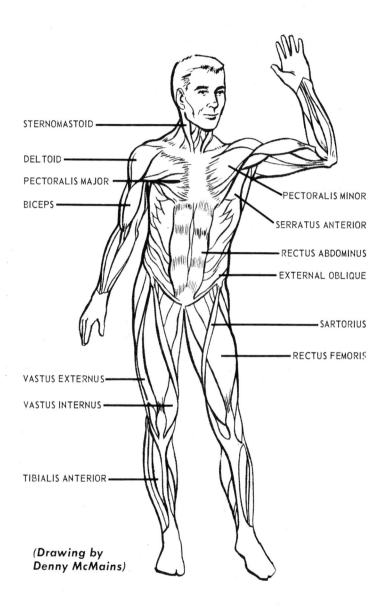

STERNOMASTOID

DELTOID

PECTORALIS MAJOR

BICEPS

PECTORALIS MINOR

SERRATUS ANTERIOR

RECTUS ABDOMINUS

EXTERNAL OBLIQUE

SARTORIUS

RECTUS FEMORIS

VASTUS EXTERNUS

VASTUS INTERNUS

TIBIALIS ANTERIOR

*(Drawing by
Denny McMains)*

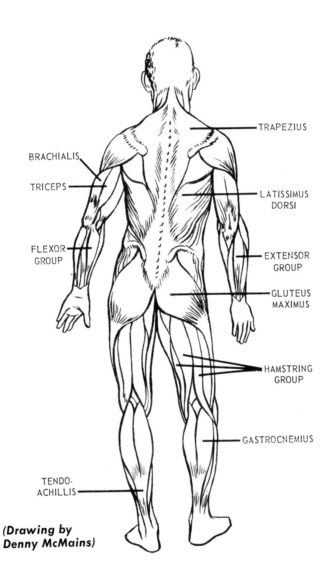

TRAPEZIUS

BRACHIALIS

TRICEPS

LATISSIMUS
DORSI

FLEXOR
GROUP

EXTENSOR
GROUP

GLUTEUS
MAXIMUS

HAMSTRING
GROUP

GASTROCNEMIUS

TENDO-
ACHILLIS

*(Drawing by
Denny McMains)*

Sugar in the body is burned to create energy during any muscular activity. First the sugar in the muscles is used, and then the sugar in the liver. The medical name for this body sugar is *glycogen*. Fat is another fuel which is consumed to create energy during exercise. Food fat is used first, followed by stored-up body fat.

Another reaction also takes place in the body during exercise. Muscle tissue actually breaks down under the strain. But whereas breaking down usually means destruction, the reverse happens with muscles—as they break down, they also build up. And since the building up is more rapid than the breaking down, the muscle is said to *hypertrophy*; that is, it becomes larger and stronger.

Muscles increase in size in direct proportion to the amount of exercise they receive. That is why any physical-fitness programme should be conducted regularly. After the body has become accustomed to resistance exercises, the more a certain routine is repeated, the better. If you exercise three times a week for two months, for example, your upper arms should show an increase of about an inch and a quarter. After four to six months they should be about two and a half inches larger than when you started. Growth can also be expected in other parts of the body, though not at the same rapid rate.

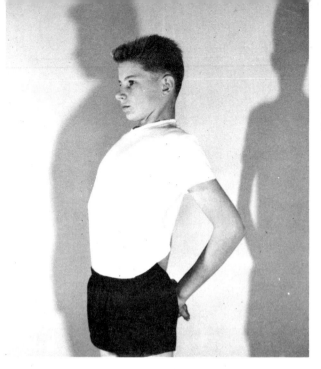

To help straighten your spine, clasp your hands behind you, bringing the chest out and shoulders back.

How to Achieve Better Posture

Do you have rounded shoulders or a sagging stomach? Do you slouch when you walk, shuffling along, looking as if you're not fit for anything more strenuous than a hot game of tiddlywinks? Poor posture is one of the great evils of soft modern living. But it can be corrected. If you really have the desire, you can make yourself hold your body straighter and firmer, looking more like a healthy human being than a scarecrow stuffed with hay.

To decide whether you need a posture-improvement programme, stand completely relaxed in front of a mirror, without holding your body any straighter than usual. Try to study yourself with complete detachment, as if you were looking at someone else. If you are not thoroughly satisfied with what you see, try the posture exercises on these pages.

To decide if you need a posture-improvement programme, study yourself in a mirror, looking for your faults.

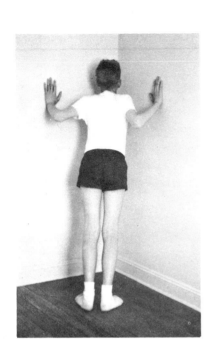

Above left: Standing in a corner, weight on heels and hands, is a fine exercise for the back.

Above: Twist palms of your hands back to work on the important shoulders.

Left: Using just the tips of your fingers, arch your back up off the floor. This is great for the back muscles.

How to Get Up in the Morning

Are you tired and listless when you get up in the morning, feeling that you'd like nothing better than to stay in bed all day? If so, you're not unusual. But if you've had eight hours' sleep, the tiredness and listlessness are probably nothing more than laziness. It is a fact that the more the average person stays in bed, the more he wants to stay in bed and the more tired he is when he drags himself, bleary-eyed and mad at the world, from between the sheets. An old saying insists, 'When you wake up, get up; and when you get up, wake up.' There is no better advice for good health.

If you're one of those fellows who stagnate in bed, make an honest comparison between yourself and the early birds among your friends. You will probably discover to your amazement that the other boys are much better athletes than you are, have more drive, get better marks in school, have more time to do more things, and have less trouble with their parents and teachers.

Want to feel better than ever before? Then hop out of bed in the morning the first time your mother calls you, ready to *live* another day instead of *dragging through* another day. If necessary at first, force yourself to get up – and you'll soon find you like it better. Then run through the exercises shown here. Take our word for it, you'll feel like a new person in a matter of just a few days.

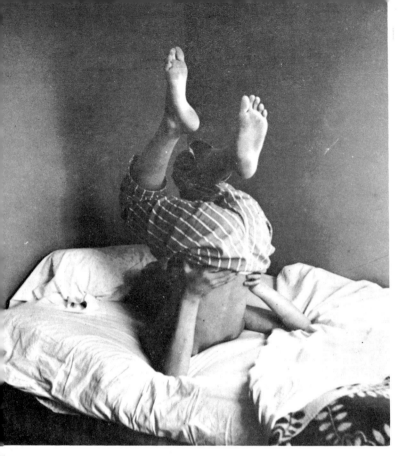

There's nothing like a bicycle
ride in the morning to limber up
the leg muscles and give you
that good-to-be-alive feeling.
Use hands to support the back.

Deep-knee bends may wind you at first, but
after a few days they'll be a breeze. Start
with a count of about ten, working up slowly.
Do each bend briskly.

22

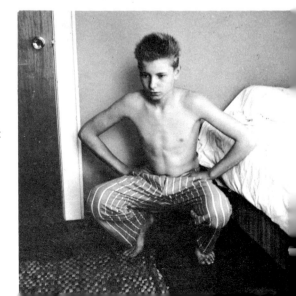

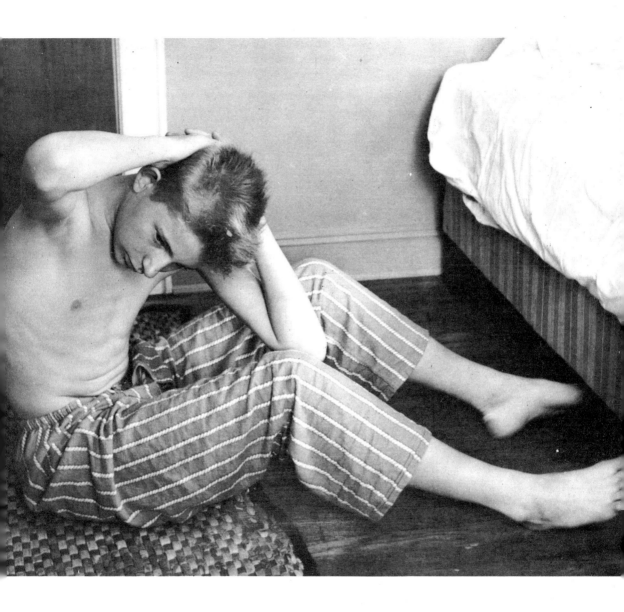

To loosen up the chest, back, and abdominal muscles, lace your fingers behind your head and swing your body to touch the left elbow to the right knee, then the right elbow to the left knee. Bend sharply each time.

Push-ups in the morning are fine for the arm and shoulder muscles.

Instead of sitting to put on your socks and shoes, take care of these jobs standing up, balancing on one foot. This will help improve your posture, too.

Below: Do this stretcher ten times for over-all fitness, touching knees to nose.

How to Exercise During the Day

It's fine to have a planned exercise programme which you follow every night or a certain number of nights a week. But if you are really sincere in wanting a healthier body and stronger muscles, it is foolish to wait until a specific time of the day to work out. You can help yourself to better health, in fact, even without a planned exercise programme, simply by performing many of the routines of daily life a little differently.

Take, for example, your morning shower. End it with a cool—*not* cold—spray of water, and then rub yourself vigorously with a rough towel. This brings a new freshness to the body and makes you feel good all over. If there is no shower in your house or apartment, rinse your chest every morning with cool water and a flannel, then rub down. The results are almost the same.

Do you have the job of putting out the rubbish? Don't consider it a chore you could do without, but gladly. Instead of carrying the bin at arm's length, hold the handle with the palm facing up and lift the bin a few times on the way to the curb, bending your arm at the elbow. Do this three or four times with each arm, and within a few weeks your biceps will be harder and bigger than ever before.

If you pass any trees with low branches on your way to school or at any other time, don't just walk on without another look. Jump up and grab a branch and chin yourself a couple of times. This brief pause will break the monotony of the walk and work wonders for your muscles.

When you come to a tree with a low branch,
jump up and grab it and chin yourself to
develop the arms.

Don't always carry your books under an arm.
Hold a book out in each hand to work on the
back and chest.

Pump your arms back and forth for the
back and chest muscles. This is an excellent
exercise you can do almost any time of day.

Once in a while try walking with one foot
on the curb and the other in the street. It's
not only fun, it's good to develop the
muscles in your thighs.

One of the very best exercises is walking. Look for ways you can walk an extra half-mile, and not for ways to avoid walking. But don't just shuffle along. Step out smartly and breathe deeply, swinging your arms rather than just letting them hang as if they were dead weights. And be sure to take stairs two at a time instead of trudging up one at a time. This is good for the entire body.

Don't drag the rubbish bin along at arm's length. Lift it a few times on the way to the curb, curling the arm. This will build your biceps in a few weeks.

27

Above left: Digging in the garden is as good for the body as any planned routine. It develops the arms, back, shoulders, chest, and legs. But stop before you're tired.

Above: If you mow the lawn, put as much arm movement into it as possible.

Left: Bend at the knees, back straight, when picking up an object you've dropped.

28

How to Set Up a Programme

Before attempting to set up a programme, you should know what the word 'exercise' means. The dictionary says that, among other things, it is 'bodily exertion for keeping the organs and functions healthy'. This definition is accurate, but it does not go far enough, for bodily exertion alone is not necessarily exercise. Medical sources give a far better meaning of the word as it is applied to body building. They say that exercise is 'the rapid and regular use of a large number of the voluntary muscles of the body–of the legs, arms, chest, back, abdomen, and neck'.

Note particularly the use of the word 'regular' in the above quotation, for regularity of training is of utmost importance in any body-building programme. Exercises conducted on a when-you-can-get-to-them basis are hardly worth the trouble, but a programme followed regularly builds and develops.

The mere free moving of a part of the body will do very little to tone or develop muscles. If, for example, you extend an arm with the fingers limp and bend the arm back and forth, touching the fingers to your shoulder, you are using muscle power. But you would have to repeat this motion perhaps scores of times to derive any real benefit from the flexing of the muscles. However, if you ball your fingers into a fist and tense the arm as you move it back and forth, this same flexing motion will tone and develop the muscles. In other words, the secret to body building is *resistance* in exercises.

Every exercise illustrated or described in this book is a resistance exercise. Some are the free-hand type, which utilize body weight or body tension for resistance. Some are with apparatus you can make or obtain at little or no cost, and some are with barbells.

Many people admire the development of men shown in physical-fitness advertisements and wish that they had enough money to buy professional equipment so that they too could build their muscles. If you have been using lack of money as an excuse, forget it; your excuse is no good. Free-hand exercises, or exercises with equipment you can make or obtain *absolutely free*, are every bit as good as those done with heavy weights.

How often should you exercise, and for what period of time? Before attempting to do even one of the easiest routines shown in this book, you should decide what you want to accomplish. If your main object is merely to tone and improve your body without necessarily increasing the size of your muscles, one or two fifteen-minute sessions a week will be enough. But if you decide that you want to build your muscles, you should plan to exercise at least three times each and every week.

The majority of boys who start physical-fitness programmes gradually lose their interest after a few weeks. This is because they either start off with a programme that is too ambitious, or because they do not have a programme at all. The few who stick at it are usually those who start off right. If you want to *continue* as well as start a programme, here are three things you should do:

1. Make a list of the exercises you plan to do, including the number of repetitions, and do each of them every session.

2. Try to get a friend to work out with you. This helps turn each session into a game, with one boy exercising while the other takes a breather.

3. Plan to work out every day, that you exercise, at the same time, instead of scheduling your exercises for 'sometime in the evening'. You can find the time if you want to badly enough.

And here are four things you should not do:

1. Do not exercise more than about fifteen minutes at a time or more than three times a week.

2. Do not let anything stand in the way of your schedule. There may be a good television show on, but forget it. Your body is more important.

3. Do not start your programme with advanced exercises. Begin slowly and progress steadily. This advice is repeated several times on the following pages, and with good reason.

4. Do not expect your muscles to pop up suddenly. It will probably be several weeks before you notice any change in your body. But whether you notice the change or not, you may be sure that, if you work out regularly, you are progressing.

How to Exercise Properly

Some people have the idea that it does little good to exercise unless the routine is continued until it hurts. This is absolutely false. Although benefits can be realized by repeating an exercise until the muscles are sore, this extreme is not necessary to acquire a good level of fitness. In fact, most physical culturists insist that far greater good can be derived from exercise by avoiding stiffness and soreness.

Many people also believe that a person who is active in sports has no need to work out further. This is true in a sense, but an important word has been left out. That word is *if*. Sports alone will keep the body in good shape, but only *if* they are the correct sports, and only *if* they are participated in regularly.

Swimming is perhaps the best all-round sport for physical fitness, exercising all the muscles of the body. But how many people can swim regularly the year round? Football and cricket and basketball are also good for certain muscles, but none of these exercises all the muscles. Cricket, for example, exercises the legs and arms, certainly when you are batting, bowling or keeping wicket. But the other important muscles of the body receive only a slight workout. The same is true of football. Football itself does not put anyone into top physical condition; instead, you have to be in shape in order to play. That is why coaches start practice sessions with callisthenics—to tone their players' muscles so that they will be able to play to the very best of their ability.

You can do many things during the day to help improve your body, as explained in the chapter beginning on page 25. But, if you decide to set up a definite programme, you should never exercise when your stomach is full. Boys often have the urge to run through their routines immediately after dinner. This practice should be avoided, since the body needs blood in the stomach while digesting food. Either exercise before dinner, stopping soon enough so you'll have time to wash before you eat, or do your workout after you have finished your home-

When you first start on an exercise programme, do not attempt to do routines as strenuous as these. Such workouts are far too difficult for most beginners.

work in the evening.

Be sure, also, that you do not overdo your exercise programme. Exercise, like everything else, can be carried to extremes. If you are just starting a programme, begin slowly with routines which demand only a little effort, working up gradually to more advanced exercises. This way, you can have fun charting and following your development.

In the beginning days of your programme, attempt only mild exercises like lying on your back and lifting the head or half push-ups. Progress comes quickly.

35

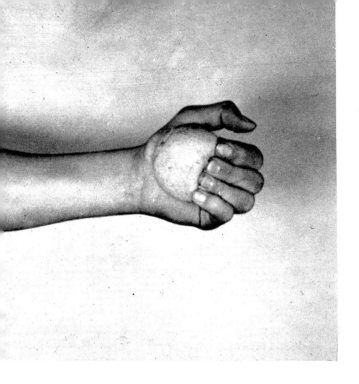

Try squeezing a rubber ball in your hand. Ten repetitions of this exercise every day would be enough to help you develop a powerful grip in a few weeks.

How to Build a Better Grip

The human hand is said to be the most marvellous mechanism ever designed. While scientists have been able to invent artificial hearts and lungs and other organs, they have never been able to fashion an instrument capable of duplicating the work of a hand. You use your hands more often than any other part of your body, but even with this constant use, strong forearms and a firm grip cannot be developed without proper exercise.

Many of the exercises described and pictured on the following pages will help mould a better grip, but a few are designed specifically for the flexor and extensor muscles of the forearm, and work only slightly on other muscles.

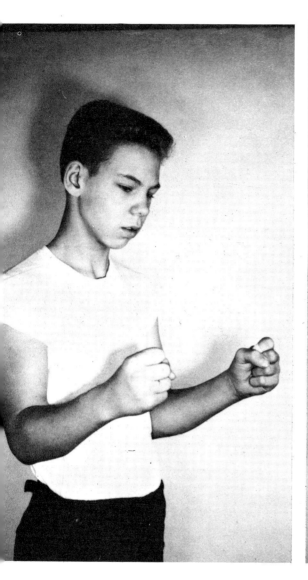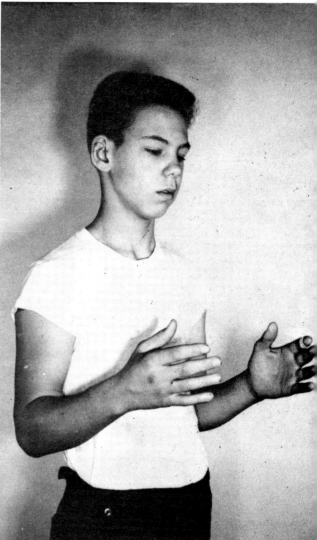

The flexing routine can be done at any time. Merely clench the hands, balling the fingers against the palms, and then extend them again. This is one of the easiest of all exercises, but it works wonders.

Perhaps the simplest of all free-hand grip exercises is the flexing routine illustrated on page 37. The beauty of this exercise is that it can be done at any time. Merely clench and unclench the hands, balling the fingers tightly and then extending them again. Repeat twenty-five times, and you will feel the effects not only in your hands, but also in your forearms. Do this every day, or several times a day, and you will soon notice a tremendous change in the power of your grip.

If you want more resistance to build an even stronger grip, try squeezing a hollow rubber ball in your hand. Ten repetitions of this exercise per day would be sufficient.

Still another grip exercise is the roller, which you can do with any weight (even your mother's old electric iron) tied to a rope about three feet long. Hold the end of the rope firmly in your hand and roll your wrist, winding the rope around your hand to lift the weight off the floor. When you have wound the weight all the way up, roll your wrist slowly in the opposite direction to lower it again. This is one of the very finest wrist and forearm exercises ever designed.

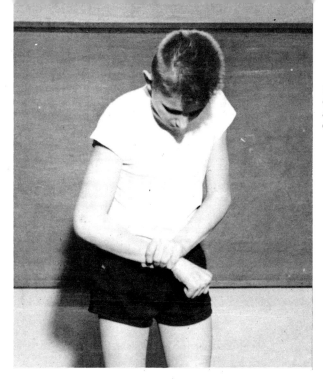

Press down on a wrist with the other hand. Tense the muscles and put plenty of effort into the exercise.

How to Strengthen Your Arms

When the average boy finally makes up his mind to undertake a body-building programme, his decision is often sparked by the fact that his upper arms look too thin and scrawny. But this lack of development of the biceps and triceps is hardly unusual. These muscles are seldom given a good workout in the routine of daily living, and a good deal of work is usually required to tone and develop them. Four free-hand exercises designed expressly for these muscles are illustrated above and on pages 40 and 41.

In the picture above, the boy is pressing down on one wrist with his other hand. This works on the biceps of one arm and triceps of the other.

Borrow one of your mother's kitchen towels for the second routine. Wrap an end of the towel round one hand and pull the free end with the other hand. The harder you pull, the more work you are making the muscles do and the faster the toning and building process.

If you have a pipe running through the basement of your house or apartment, use it for chinning. This is one of the best free-hand arm exercises, since the body weight is used for resistance. Chin both with the knuckles pointed out and with them pointed in. This works on the triceps as well as the biceps, toning and building the arms rapidly.

Pumping the arms back and forth with resistance also works well to build up muscle tissue. Pump with the knuckles pointed in the first time and with them facing out the next time.

Wrap a kitchen towel around one hand and pull hard with the other hand. Those biceps will really pop!

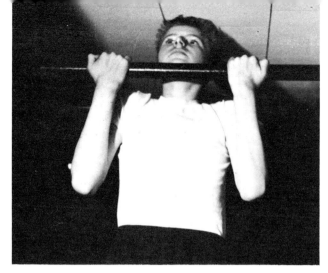

Chin yourself on a pipe somewhere in the apartment or
house, using weight of your body for resistance.

Flex your arms to stretch and tone the biceps. This is a simple workout, but
it develops muscle tissue.

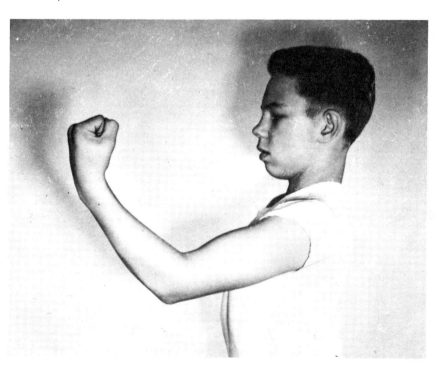

How to Develop Your Shoulders

The shoulder riser shown in the photographs on the opposite page is one of the easiest free-hand exercises illustrated in this book. Executed in proper stages, however, it can be one of the best for conditioning the deltoid muscles of the shoulders, at the same time working on the pectoralis major and serratus anterior muscles of the chest.

To do the shoulder riser, merely sit on the floor, legs extended and close together. Place your hands next to your hips and push up, lifting the buttocks and thighs off the floor. Repeat at least ten times during every workout. As you progress in your programme, place a weight of some type in your lap when doing the exercise.

The push-up shown on pages 44 and 45 is also excellent for the shoulders. Done correctly, this exercise is started in the prone position. Push straight up from the floor, holding your back stiff, and then lower yourself until your nose touches the mat. Do not allow any other part of your body to contact the mat during the exercise. Beginners should not attempt more than ten push-ups during the first week.

Thirty or thirty-five push-ups in any session should be about the limit of progression. If further resistance is desired at this point, a sandbag or other weight may be placed across the shoulders. Keep this extra weight light at first.

The shoulder riser is one of the best exercises for toning and conditioning the deltoid muscles quickly.

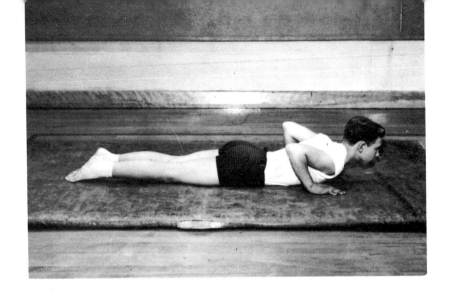

Start the push-up exercise by lying face down on the floor or mat, legs extended and held close together.

Push straight up from the floor, holding your back stiff and stomach in, weight on the toes and hands.

Raise yourself to arms' length, still keeping the body stiff and straight,

and then lower your body until only your nose touches the floor or mat.
This is one of the best all-round free-hand exercises.

How to Work on Your Neck

The neck is one of the most difficult sections of the body to exercise without resistance apparatus. However, there are three basic free-hand routines which can be used well. One is the roller, in which you merely roll your head around and up and down. This gentle action loosens and stretches the trapezius muscles at the back of the neck as well as the sternomastoid muscles in the front. The exercise can be more effective, building as well as toning, if you strain against the rolling and dipping motion.

A second exercise is the dipper, in which the arms are used to provide resistance. Lace your fingers behind your head and pull as you dip your head forward and backward. The more pressure behind the arms, the more effective the exercise.

Any boy who can do the bridge, as shown on the opposite page, is considered to have a strong neck. Lie flat on your back and then raise your body so that it is balanced only on the feet and the back of the head. Beginners should push up with their arms during the first two or three weeks, so that there will not be too much strain on the neck. After the neck and back muscles are strong enough, so that the exercise can be done without using the hands, more resistance may be added by placing a book or some other object on the stomach. Further resistance weights may be added over the months, but progress should be slow and steady.

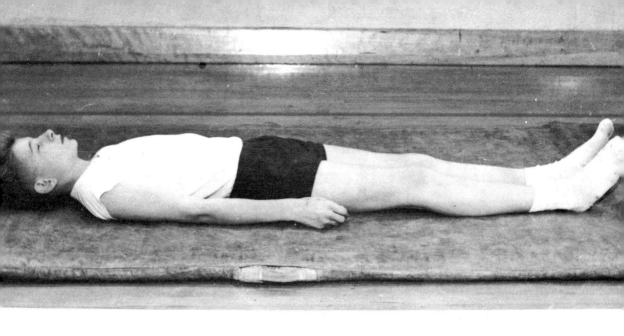

The bridge is a difficult exercise for the majority of beginners, but after a few weeks most boys are able to do it without using their hands as starters. Five repetitions of this exercise would be enough.

In the dipper exercise, lace your fingers behind the head and pull as you dip the head forward and back.

How to Broaden Your Chest

There is probably not a boy in the British Isles or the Commonwealth or any of the other highly developed countries of the world who has not at some time thought about improving his body. The muscles which are usually considered most are those of the arms and chest, since it is generally considered more 'manly' to have mighty arms and a deep chest. However, thinking alone is hardly enough. Powerful legs can be built through walking and by playing running games, since bodily weight offers the necessary resistance. But since the arms and chest do not normally have bodily resistance working against them in the routine motions of daily living, it is necessary to have specific, well-planned exercises for these muscles.

If your primary objective is muscle-building rather than general physical fitness, the fastest and most effective way to work on the pectoralis major and serratus anterior muscles of the chest is through the use of resistance apparatus. While such apparatus will produce results faster, they may also be realized through free-hand exercises programmed properly and followed conscientiously.

One good chest exercise you might try is called the pumper. Extend your arms in front of you, with the hands either open or clenched, and quickly snap the elbows back as far as they will go. The natural tendency is to exhale as the arms piston back. Overcome this impulse and, instead, inhale deeply on the backward stroke, exhaling as you bring your arms forward again to the starting position. Repeat this exercise twenty-five to thirty times, working vigorously on each backward stroke, and you will feel those chest muscles beginning to stretch.

Another excellent free-hand chest exercise which many physical culturists recommend is done by clasping the hands palm-to-palm in front of the chest and pressing them together with jerking motions. Very little pressure is required with this exercise, and the force should come from the upper arms rather than the forearms. With each repetition you will feel the pectoralis major muscles contract. This contraction, over a prolonged period, results in more muscle tissue.

Here is one of the best free-hand chest exercises. Clasp your hands palm-to-palm in front of the chest and press them together with a quick jerking motion.

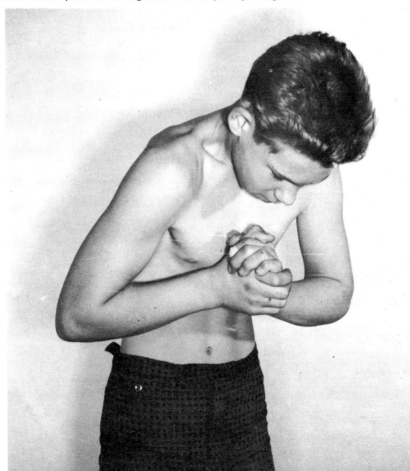

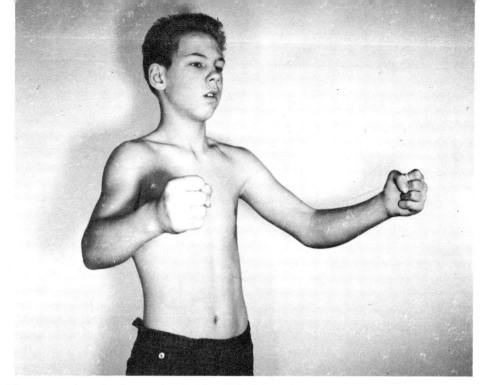

The pumper is a simple exercise, but it will build up the chest muscles quickly. Start by holding your arms out, with the hands either open or closed, and then piston the elbows back as far as they will go.

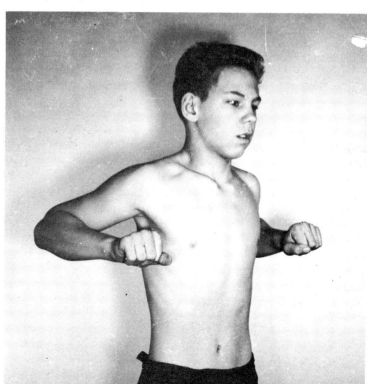

How to Flatten Your Stomach

Experience has proved that a large percentage of the boys who decide to undertake physical-fitness programmes usually concentrate most of their efforts on the arms and chest and almost ignore the other muscles. This is a peculiar situation, for the abdominal area is one of the most important in the entire body, and a deep chest and well-conditioned legs should be joined to a mid-section which is equally fit.

The main reason for this lack of attention to the abdomen by so many boys seems to be that it is necessary to work hard in order to tone these muscles properly. Also, when a boy attempts to build as well as condition his muscles, it is obvious that a certain amount of work spent on chest, legs, or arms will produce more noticeable results than an equal amount of work expended on the midsection. However, no programme can be truly complete unless all the important sections of the body are given proper attention.

Among the most important and beneficial free-hand exercise to strengthen the rectus and external oblique muscles of the abdomen is

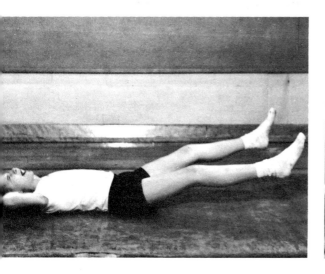 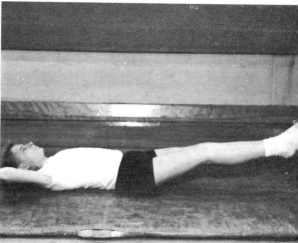

There is no denying that the leg lift is a difficult exercise, but it is one of the best
for the abdomen and back. To begin, raise legs high, then lower them slowly toward the
mat without bending at the knees.
The leg-lift routine is even more beneficial if the legs are spread on the way down
and brought together again during the holding count. Lie still for a few seconds after each
repetition, relaxing the muscles.

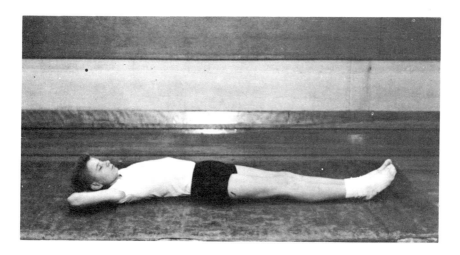

The reverse bridge is a fine free-hand exercise for the back as well as the abdomen, but it is rough to do. Hold the legs up as shown, then pull with the arms to raise both the thighs and chest off the mat.

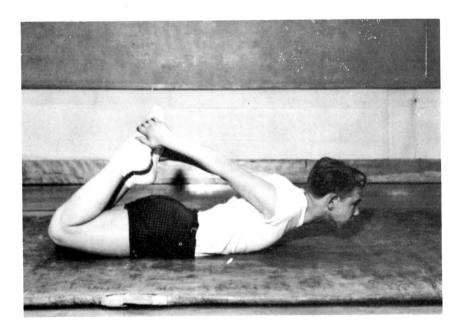

the leg lift. The mere thought of this exercise makes many boys groan, and it is the one routine in which there are so many cheaters during group workouts, bending their legs at the knees instead of holding them straight. But regardless of the moans and groans, any well-balanced conditioning programme should include leg lifts during every exercise period.

The leg-lift technique illustrated in this chapter is the correct way to execute the exercise so that it will give the abdominal and back muscles the proper workout. Note that the boy lifts his legs high, keeping his feet together, and then lowers them slowly. The greatest benefit is derived by holding the legs raised about three to six inches above the floor for a count of ten or more. Still further benefit comes from spreading the legs during the count and then bringing them together again before dropping them to the floor. Beginners should not repeat this exercise more than ten times, slowly working up to fifteen and a holding count of fifteen or twenty.

The reverse bridge is another fine stomach exercise which also helps to strengthen the shoulder and back muscles. Lie face down on the mat, hands back and holding the legs. The exercise is done by arching the back and pulling with the hands, raising the chest and thighs off the mat. This is one of the most difficult exercises, but it pays big dividends in conditioning the body. Beginners should limit themselves to not more than five repetitions of the routine.

The sit-ups and toe swings pictured on the next page are also excellent for back and stomach muscles. Note that in each case the boy keeps his legs flat on the mat, without bending his knees.

Sit-ups are among the best routines for
strengthening the rectus and external oblique
muscles of the abdomen. If more resistance
is desired for faster development, hold a light
weight behind your head.

Toe swings not only strengthen abdominal
muscles but also stretch and tone them. You may
not be able to touch your toes at first, but
after a few sessions the muscles will be much
looser and more flexible.

How to Build Better Legs

The legs are exercised more often in the course of daily life than any other part of the body, and physical culturists all agree that walking is one of the very best exercises. The difficulty with normal everyday walking, however, is that the knees are not bent sharply enough to tone and condition the muscles to their fullest extent and loosen the important tendons.

One of the best free-hand exercises for the legs is the knee pump shown in the pictures on page 58. To do the exercise, balance your weight on the hands and toes, then shoot one leg back while bringing the other one forward, bending both legs at the knees. Keep the legs in constant motion during the routine, pumping them back and forth as rapidly as possible. Do a count of ten each day for the first two weeks, fifteen for the third week, and twenty thereafter. This is a simple exercise, but it will take the wind out of you if you are not in the best of condition. A count of not more than twenty-five should be the maximum during any workout.

Another good leg exercise is the sitting knee pump shown on pages 60 and 61. This appears to be even easier than the knee pump, but it is actually a bit more difficult. Whereas in the knee pump it is necessary

The knee pump limbers and tones all the muscles of the legs far better than walking ever could. Keep both legs in constant motion throughout the routine.

only to pump the legs, with the weight balanced on the hands and toes, the sitting knee pump requires a lifting action in which the weight of the entire leg is supported wholly by the thighs and hips.

In the sitting knee pump, one knee at a time is brought up sharply as high as possible toward the chest. Alternate legs during the exercise, pumping first with one leg and then with the other. Do a count of ten with each leg the first week; twelve the second; and fifteen thereafter. If your legs are extremely limber and well developed, you may work up to a count of twenty or more after a period of time, but this number is neither advisable nor necessary for the average boy whose prime concern is conditioning.

For general limbering of the hips and legs, nothing beats the old bicycle exercise pictured on this page. To do this routine, support your weight on your shoulders, with the hips and legs vertically off the floor or mat. You may take some of the weight off the shoulders by holding your back or buttocks up with your hands. The legs are pumped in a small circle, exactly as if you were riding a bicycle, bringing the knees

No free-hand conditioning exercise for the legs has ever been devised that can take the place of the old bicycle routine. The faster and harder you ride the bicycle, the better— but don't keep it up too long.

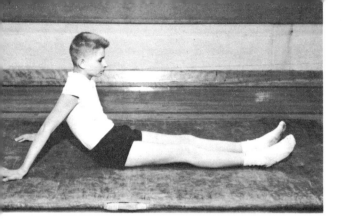

While the sitting knee pump appears to be even easier than the knee pump, it is really more difficult. Start in the sitting position, pumping one leg at a time as high and as close to your chest as possible.

down as far as possible on the up stroke. Continue riding the bicycle until your legs feel loose, but stop before you are tired and breathing too deeply. No exercise should be carried to the point of exhaustion, because the strain on the heart may become too great. One difficulty with the bicycle is that some boys continue it too long for their own good.

Still another excellent old-fashioned free-hand exercise for the legs is the deep-knee bend. This, like the bicycle, is easy to do. Unlike the bicycle, though, you always know beyond doubt when you've had enough.

Start the deep-knee bends with hands on hips. As you bend the knees, swing your hands to the front for better balance. At the deepest part of the bend, your weight should be entirely on the toes and balls of the feet. Many boys try to do this exercise while remaining flat-footed. This defeats its purpose, since the muscles and tendons in the instep do not receive their full share of the workout.

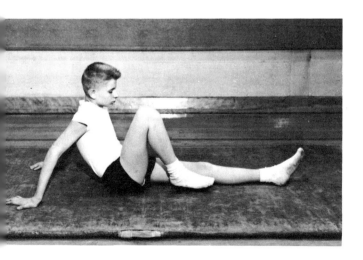

Another terrific old-timer, the deep-knee bend uses body weight for resistance.
Have your weight on the toes and balls of the feet at the deepest point of the bend, hands
stretched out to maintain balance.

How to Work Out With a Friend

One of the biggest drawbacks to an individual exercise programme is the problem of loneliness. No matter how sincere a boy may be in the desire to tone and condition his body, his progress will suffer if he attempts to do it entirely on his own. This applies whether the programme is designed either for free-hand workouts or for apparatus. To get the most out of any session, it is advisable for at least two or three boys to work out together. One boy should go through a certain routine while the others are resting.

Hand-to-hand combative exercises with a friend should not be overlooked, either. These require no equipment, not even a mat, and most of them can be done either indoors or outdoors. Hand-to-hand combative exercises are fun to do, and they have the added advantage of teaching better balance, better timing, and better co-ordination.

When selecting a partner for hand-to-hand combative exercises, do not pick a boy who is smaller and lighter than you are. If you know beforehand that you will be able to win almost every time, without giving your best efforts, you will be helping the other fellow condition his muscles to the point where he may someday beat you. Instead, try to find a boy about your own size and weight, or perhaps one who is even a bit larger and heavier. This way, you will do your own body the most good.

Remember, above all, that consistent winning is not necessarily the object in hand-to-hand combative exercises. Be just as willing to try the games at which the other fellow is better. By following this method – and following it sincerely – you will both get more fun out of the exercises, and you will also discover that in time you may lose in some of your specialties while beating your partner in some of his. When this happens, you will both know that you have improved your bodies as well as your playing techniques and that you are on your way towards better fitness.

The back-to-back lift is a good, all-around hand-to-hand combative exercise. Stand with your back firmly against your partner's, arms locked as shown. First one boy lifts by bending over, then the other lifts.

The stick-pull is excellent for the whole body, from shoulders to legs. Draw a line
on the ground with your toe; and then, with both partners holding the stick, each tries to
pull the other over the line.

65

Hand wrestling is great for timing. Neither foot may be moved; try to make your partner lose his balance.

The wrist-curl moulds a good grip. Lace fingers with your partner, knuckles up, and try to force him down.

In the stick-drop exercise, each boy tries to keep the stick from turning in his hands as it is lowered.

To do the arm-pull routine, one boy holds his fists together and the other attempts to pull them apart.

In the donkey-drag, hold hands with your friend like this and try to pull him over a line on the ground.

Indian wrestling is an old-time favourite. Each boy works to flip his partner over when they lock legs.

How to Work Out With a Broom

An ordinary kitchen broom can be used with excellent results in exercise programmes. Three good exercises are illustrated on these pages. With just a little thought you can devise others which may be integrated into your workouts.

The photograph opposite shows how a broom can be used to develop the wrists and forearms. Hold the broom as far out on the handle as possible, allowing the bristle end to rest on the floor. Then, with wrist action alone, raise the broom until it is approximately parallel with the floor. Repeat this exercise five times daily with each arm for a week or two, and then gradually work up to a count of ten. As your wrists become stronger, hold the broom handle farther towards the end, so that the forearm cannot be used as a lever to raise it. To provide still more resistance, a book or two may be added to the broom. Do not become too optimistic in adding weights, however, because only a few extra ounces will feel 'like a ton'.

Another wrist exercise with a broom is the twister shown on page 70. Hold the broom in front of your body and twist forward with one hand and backward with the other, clenching the handle tightly to prevent it from turning in your hands. Alternate the twisting action to exercise both hands equally. As a word of caution, do not continue this exercise longer than a minute or two in the beginning stages. If it is continued beyond this time—assuming that you are really putting pressure into the twisting action—you will probably end up

Using wrist action alone, raise the broom parallel with the floor. Do five times daily with each arm.

For more resistance, balance a book or two on the broom. The effect of this extra weight is amazing.

with a set of painful blisters on the palms of your hands.

A broom exercise which works on the wrists, arms, and shoulders equally is the stretcher, illustrated below. To do this, hold the broom above and behind your head, with the arms bent at right angles. Twist one hand forward and the other one backward, as in the twister, at the same time pulling out to the sides along the length of the handle. Continue this pulling and twisting action for a minute or so and you will feel your flexor, extensor, and biceps muscles stretching and aching.

Still another broom exercise, which is not illustrated, is the step-over. Hold the broom in both hands, step over it, twist it up and around your back without loosening your grip or allowing the handle to turn in your hands. This is a good one for the shoulders.

In the twister exercise, you twist one hand forward and the other backward. Do not let the handle turn. For wrists, arms, and shoulders, hold the broom behind your head, pulling and twisting with both hands.

How to Work Out With Chairs

When you have worked out with free-hand exercises for about a month, you may want more resistance to build as well as condition your muscles. If so, try borrowing a couple of your mother's kitchen chairs for use in your sessions.

A good chair exercise for the arms, shoulders, chest, and abdomen is the swinger shown in the photographs on page 72. Stand beside the chair and hold it lightly at the lower part of the back rest, using just the curled tips of your fingers. Swing the chair up from the floor, keeping the arms straight, and hold it extended for a count of five. Repeat the exercise up to ten times during the first week, and then gradually increase not only the repetitions but also the length of time the chair is held extended.

For stronger wrists and forearms, you might also add to your routine the exercise shown on the top of page 73. Kneel behind the chair and, grasping the legs as close to the floor as possible, swing it up until your arms are straight out. As with the swinger, hold the chair extended for a count of five during the first week.

The dipper exercise, which is also illustrated on page 73, builds the arms, chest, and shoulders much faster than normal push-ups from the floor, since it is possible to dip the body lower and give the muscles a more strenuous workout pushing up again.

Before starting the dipper, place the chairs just far enough for the shoulders to fit between them. Wrap your fingers around the sides of the chairs, as shown in the photographs, and push up with the heels of your hands, keeping your body stiff and straight. Repeat up to ten times each session during the first week, and then slowly increase the count to a maximum of twenty-five.

The chinner illustrated in the photographs on page 74 is fine for developing the chest, back, shoulder, and arm muscles. Place a broom handle or some other strong bar across the tops of two chairs, making sure that they will not tip under your weight. Assume a sitting position between the chairs and, grasping the bar, pull up and chin on the bar. The exercise has more value if the body is held straight, resting only on the heels. However, it is advisable to work up to this advanced technique in easy stages.

To do the chair-swinger exercise, stand behind the chair and hold it lightly at the lower part of the back rest. Swing the chair up from the floor, keeping the arms straight, and hold it for a count of five.

ove and right: Here's a chair exercise that builds the ʼsts and forearms better than most free-hand workouts. ›m a kneeling position, grasp the legs as close to the ɔr as possible, then swing the chair out straight, holding ɔr a count of five.

Below: The dipper exercise between two chairs is a variation of the push-up, but it can provide a far better workout because the body may be dipped below the seats of the chairs. Note position of the hands.

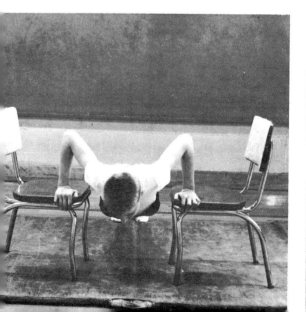

In the early stages of the chinner between chairs, assume a sitting position as shown. It is more difficult, but far better, to do the exercise with the body straight, weight resting entirely on the heels.

How to Work Out With Sandbags

A pair of bags made of canvas or some other strong material and filled with sand make excellent weights for exercising. Using such bags, you can go through almost the entire routine of weight-training exercises without the expense of buying barbells. Make the bags about eight inches wide and a foot or fourteen inches long. Stitch up three sides on a sewing machine, fill them with eight or ten pounds of sand, and then sew the remaining side up. For ease of handling, you may tie lengths of clothesline firmly around the ends, looping the rope to make handles.

The pictures on page 76 show three sets of exercises which may be done with sandbag weights. In the top photographs, the boy is curling a bag to work on his wrists, arms, and chest. In the middle pictures, he is extending a bag out parallel with the floor to develop his arms, shoulders, and back. In the bottom set, he is pushing the bag up from his head in another arm-and-shoulder exercise.

The photographs on page 78 illustrate the way a sandbag may be used to add more resistance to sit-ups than is possible when they are done by the free-hand method. This exercise is good for the abdomen and back. If the weight is so heavy that it upsets your balance, hook your toes under a chair for better leverage.

The exercise shown on page 77 is designed expressly for the abdomen. It is the next step beyond free-hand leg lifts.

Top: Curls with a sandbag build up muscle tissue much faster than those done by the free-hand method. *Centre:* Here's a good routine for the arms, shoulders, and back. *Bottom:* As a variation, also try this exercise to harden and develop the arms and shoulders.

On page 79 are two other sandbag exercises. In the first, the bag is snatched off the floor and brought up over the head in a smooth motion. This develops the back, abdomen, and shoulders. The final two photographs depict a shoulder exercise which builds shoulder muscles in the shortest possible time. Raise the weights straight out from your sides and hold them at arms' length as long as possible, then lower them slowly.

Leg lifts with a sandbag across the insteps are difficult, but they build hard stomach muscles.

Sit-ups with a sandbag held firmly under your head are great for the muscles of the abdomen and back. If the extra weight upsets your balance, making the legs rise, hook your toes under a chair for leverage.

Top: You can flatten your stomach and add inches to your chest and shoulders with this sandbag routine. *Bottom:* Here's another sandbag exercise for the chest, arms, and back. Do at least five repetitions daily.

How to Work Out With Bicycle Tubes

If you would like to have most of the exercise advantages of a set of barbells without the disadvantage of high cost, pick up a couple of discarded bicycle inner tubes from your local bicycle repair shop. The owner probably will not charge you for the tubes, since they are of absolutely no use to him. However, what may be trash to one person can often prove valuable to another, and these old bicycle tubes will help to give you muscles as hard and as strong as any you could develop with the best professional equipment.

When selecting the tubes, it is a good idea to pick out two that are about the same size, so that they will provide equal resistance during your exercise sessions. In addition to the inner tubes, you will need only a piece of pipe or a broom handle to make your home gymnasium complete.

For a complete workout, do each of the exercises shown on these pages. Try to repeat each ten times, but if one or two of the routines prove too difficult, do not strain to reach ten. Start with a smaller number of repetitions and slowly increase the count. Or if you find that the tubes do not offer enough resistance, simply twist them once around your hand. You will be amazed by the increased resistance. You will also be amazed by the way the inner tube workouts take off weight if you are too fat or put it on if you are too thin. And watch how those muscles begin to harden and grow!

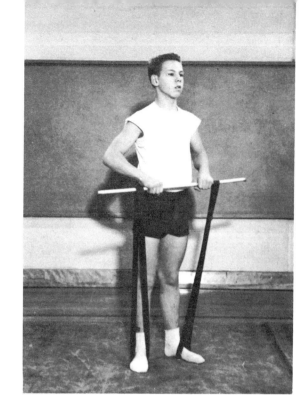

To do overhead presses with inner tubes, stand firmly on each of the tubes and loop them over a piece of pipe or broom handle. Either push up from shoulders or return to starting position after each press.

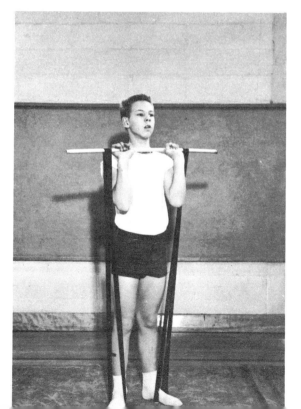

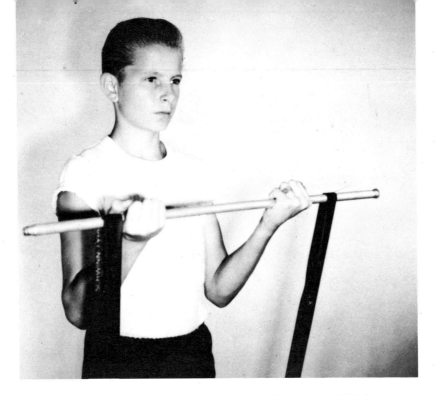

To curl the tubes, step in the loops as in the overhead press. This is one of the best resistance exercises for the biceps. Do not jerk the bar but curl it up and down slowly and smoothly for best results.

To do the reverse curl, stand in the tubes as before, but hold the handle with the knuckles pointed up. This works on the triceps as well as flexor and extensor groups. Do both types of curls each workout.

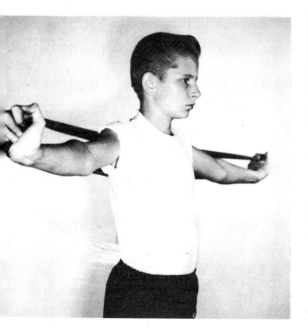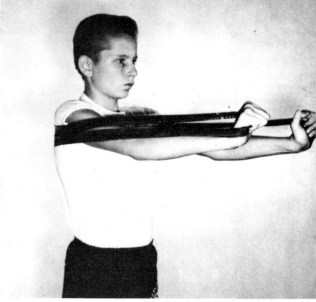

For the deltoid muscles of the shoulders, stretch a tube behind your back and then swing the arms forward as shown. For still better results, pump both arms forward and back after the tube is stretched.

Left: Stretch a tube in front of you for a mighty chest. *Right:* This is a good one for arms and back.

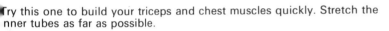

Try this one to build your triceps and chest muscles quickly. Stretch the inner tubes as far as possible.

Above: Bob your head up and down to work on the neck muscles. *Below:* This is for the arms and shoulders.

How to Work Out With Barbells

If you already own a set of barbells and would like to work out with them, bear in mind that there is a great difference between weight *training* and weight *lifting*. Weight lifting is a form of competition in which the performer lifts a maximum weight in a single lift. By contrast, in weight training the performer lifts a below-maximum weight a number of times, not for exhibition or in competition, but to build his body. Many experts frown upon the use of barbells or dumbbells for boys because many of them try to 'show off', attempting to lift more than they should. This can cause more harm than good, placing too great a strain on the muscles as well at the vital organs of the body.

To determine the amount of weight you should use for your own particular stage of development, it would be wise to experiment over a period of days in different exercises, since each set of muscles has its own limitations. Finally select the amount of weight for each routine which will allow you to do eight repetitions without too much strain. After you are able to handle a certain weight with comparative ease during a routine, add further weights in slow stages, putting on no more than another five pounds at a time. You may feel that it is foolish to work out with weights well below your total lifting capacity, but for your own good you should remember that it is the *repetition* of an exercise which counts most in body building.

When working out with barbells, do each routine smoothly and without jerking movements. Remember also that proper breathing is important, inhaling and holding your breath during the exercise and exhaling after it has been completed.

Spread your legs slightly when doing presses, to be sure your balance is good. Hold the bar firmly and press straight up. Repeat eight times only if you can do the exercise ten times without undue strain.

You can press the most weight when lying prone, but for safety you should stay below your maximum. It is good to have a friend with you, handing you the barbells to start and taking them when you're finished.

Do curls slowly and smoothly if you are seeking maximum results in building the biceps, keeping the elbows away from the body. Reverse curls, with the knuckles pointed up, work more on the triceps.

Squats develop leg muscles quickly, but lean forward as you go down to preserve balance.

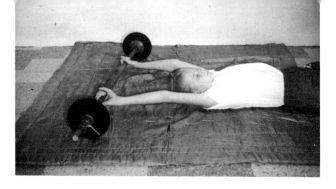

Pull-overs develop arm and shoulder muscles. Lie on the mat with barbells behind your head. Pull them up over your chest, dip them down, press up, then lower them to your thighs. For maximum results, lift barbells from the thighs back to starting position.

90

How to Start Off Right

The first few weeks of a physical-fitness programme are the most important ones by far. During this period either good or bad exercise habits are developed which often influence the success of the entire programme. Experts have estimated that as many as 75 per cent of the people who start programmes with good intentions find one excuse after another to miss exercise sessions after two or three weeks, while still others fall off after another week or two. Experience has indicated that many boys discontinue because they start off with programmes that are too advanced for their bodies.

To be truly effective, a physical-fitness programme should be continued for six to eight months at the very least, with workouts scheduled for every Monday, Wednesday and Friday. It should also be started slowly and carefully, with exercises that are not too much work. Any boy who attempts to curl a fifty-pound barbell fifteen or more times during his first workout, with the idea of fast development, will proably realize no development at all. Instead, after a few sessions, he will undoubtedly find a more enjoyable way to spend his time.

Every exercise shown in this book is good for the body. However, just as exercise that is too strenuous is not advisable, so it is also inadvisable to start off without a definite programme. Before you attempt to do any of the other exercises illustrated, it would be better to concentrate on the routines shown in the charts on pages 92 and 93 for at least two weeks. This applies whether you plan to do either free-hand exercises or exercises with resistance apparatus. Do each of the exercises not more than ten times during the first week, and not more than twelve times during the second week. If you are not able to reach this number of repetitions without too much effort, add another week or two to your preliminary conditioning period.

Routine 1—Start with your legs spread comfortably and bend deep. Do not become discouraged if you are unable to touch your toes at first.

Routine 2—Try to touch your toes in this sit-up exercise without bending your knees.

Routine 3—Crouch low, hands on the floor, and then spring up, spreading your arms and legs. Come down again in a crouch.

Routine 4—Keep your body stiff during push-ups, do not allow it to

touch the floor as you go down.

Routine 5–Do the duck walk five steps, then run in place ten steps before going down again.

Routine 6–Swivel your body first in one direction, and then the other, touching elbows to knees.

Routine 7–Lift your head and legs off the floor, hands clasped behind your back.

Routine 8–Either keep hands on hips in deep-knee bends or hold the arms extended in front as you go down, to preserve balance.

93

Glossary of Physical Fitness Terms

ABDOMEN–The section of the body between the lower chest and the groin.

BARBELL–Weights used in weight lifting and weight training. The bar is usually made of steel and is several feet long. The bells are disc-shaped weights.

BENCH PRESS–An exercise performed with apparatus, in which the performer lies on a bench and presses weights straight up from his chest.

BICEPS–The muscles on the front of the upper arm.

BODY BUILDING–The science of improving the physique by exercise.

BULK–The term used to describe added muscle weight.

CARDIORESPIRATORY ENDURANCE–The ability to perform an activity that puts a burden on breathing rather than on muscle power. Swimming, basketball, and soccer require this type of endurance.

CHEATING–A method used by weight lifters to lift heavy weights at the expense of proper body-building technique.

CLEAN and JERK–A weight-lifting technique in which the barbells are snatched off the floor and jerked up over the performer's head.

COMBATIVE EXERCISES–Exercises conducted with a partner and without using apparatus.

CRAMPING–Exercises which concentrate on contracting muscles without working a full range.

CURL–An exercise in which the arms are curled to contract the biceps and triceps.

DEEP-KNEE BEND–An exercise in which the performer stands upright and then bends his knees to a crouching position.

DEFINITION–Quality rather than quantity of muscle formation. Small well-toned muscles can often be more beneficial than bulky muscles.

DELTOID–A shoulder muscle.

DUMBBELLS–Small hand weights used in weight training.

GASTROCNEMIUS–The large muscle at the back of the lower leg.

LATISSIMUS DORSI–A lower back muscle.

LEG RAISE–An exercise in which the performer lies on his back and raises his legs from the floor.

MUSCULAR ENDURANCE–Acquired strength which allows a performer to repeat a muscular effort a number of times or over an extended period.

MUSCLE-BOUND–A misused term often applied to people who have well-developed muscles. However, it is possible to have bound, or cramped, muscles through overexertion brought on by incorrect training methods.

MUSCLE CONTROL–The ability to flex certain muscles independently of other muscles.

PECTORALIS MAJOR–A chest muscle.

PULL-OVER–An exercise in which the performer lies on his back with the barbells extended behind his head. Keeping his arms straight, he pulls the weights off the floor and raises them until they are above his chest.

RECTUS–The muscles which cover the front of the body from below the chest to the groin.

RECTUS FEMORIS–The large muscles on the front of the thigh.

REVERSE CURL–Same as the Curl, but with the knuckles in front.

SETS – A certain number of repetitions of an exercise.

SIT-UP – An exercise in which the performer lies on his back and raises his body to a sitting position.

SPECIALIZED SCHEDULES – Exercise programmes designed to build certain sections of the body.

TRICEPS – The muscles on the back of the upper arm.

WEIGHT-LIFTING – A competitive sport in which a contestant lifts a maximum amount of weight in a single lift. Weight-lifting should be avoided by boys, since it may do more harm than good.

WEIGHT-TRAINING – A body-building programme in which a below-maximum weight is lifted a number of times.

WORKOUT – A training session.